Acknowledgements

Editing text:
Alice Knigsnorth
Design:
Toghrul Manafov

Published by Rauf Khalilov 2024
Copyright © 2024
First edition.
The author asserts the moral right under the Copyright, Design and Patents Act 1988 to be identified as the author of his work.
All rights reserved. No part of this publication may be reproduced, stored in a retrieval system or transmitted in any form or by any means without the prior consent of the author, nor be otherwise circulated in any form of binding or cover other than that with which it is published and without a similar condition being imposed on
the subsequent purchaser.

ISBN: 978-1-8383500-9-3

LEARN TALYSH

In memory of my beloved paternal grandparents, Munavvar Aghayeva and Haji Eynali Khalilov, whose love and guidance nurtured my passion for the Talysh language and whose wisdom and dedication have inspired my journey into the depths of our cultural heritage.

INTRODUCTION

In the dynamic Republic of Azerbaijan, nestled between the Caucasus Mountains and the Caspian Sea, unfolds a story of diversity and unity. Recognized as the Land of Fire, Azerbaijan boasts a rich history with a multitude of ethnicities, all contributing to its multicultural tapestry.

Guided by the visionary leadership of former President Heyder Aliyev and his son, President Ilham Aliyev, Azerbaijan embraces the beauty of its multiculturalism. Both leaders champion values of unity, inclusivity, and mutual respect, fostering an environment where every ethnic group is encouraged to preserve and celebrate their unique cultural identities. President Ilham Aliyev once stated, "We are proud of our multicultural values and our ethnic diversity. This diversity is our strength, giving us a unique identity."

Amidst these diverse ethnicities is the Talysh people, referring to themselves as the "Talushon." Predominantly residing in the southeast of Azerbaijan and the northern regions of Iran, the Talysh people maintain a deep connection to their ancestral lands. Estimates suggest up to 600,000 Talysh people live across 350 towns and villages in Azerbaijan, with an additional 165,000 in northern Iran, namely Gilan and Ardabil. Smaller populations reside in Russia and Kazakhstan.

Renowned for their centuries-old heritage, artistic endeavors, hospitality, and craftsmanship, the Talysh people contribute significantly to Azerbaijani society. Through their language, spoken across eight cities, including Astara, Lerik, Lankaran, and Masally, we discover a bridge connecting the past with the present—a world of expression, tradition, and communication.

In these pages, we invite you to delve into the Talysh language, exploring its grammar, vocabulary, and unique features. The language comprises three major dialects: Southern Talyshi, Central Talyshi, and Northern Talyshi, each offering slightly different expressions.

Explore this captivating language to gain insights into the Talysh people's way of life, customs, folklore, and enduring spirit. Together, let's celebrate the Talysh people, enriching your linguistic repertoire and expanding your understanding and appreciation for the diverse tapestry thriving across the Republic of Azerbaijan.

CHAPTER I
THE ALPHABET

A B C Ç D E Ə F Q Ğ H X I İ J K L M N O P R S Ş T Ü V Y Z

The Talysh alphabet plays a vital role in preserving and expressing the unique Talysh language. In this chapter, we will delve into the Talysh alphabet, which consists of 29 letters, with 22 consonants and 7 vowels. Each letter carries its own distinct sound and pronunciation. Let's explore the individual letters and their corresponding sounds in detail.

A:

The letter "A" in Talysh has the sound of "a" as in "glass". However, it is pronounced shorter, resembling the "a" sound in words like "blood" or "much".

Examples:

- Asb   –   Horse
- Amu   –   Uncle
- Arzu   –   Desire

B:

The letter "B" represents the sound of "b" as in "bravo".

Examples:

- Bala   –   Child
- Bəv   –   Brow
- Bebəfo   –   Unfaithful

C:

The letter "C" in Talysh is pronounced as "j" in English, resembling the "j" sound in words like "jacket".

Examples:

- Cəvon – Young
- Camaat – People
- Cəsarət – Bravery

Ç:

The letter "Ç" produces the sound of "ch", as in "chocolate".

Examples:

- Çiç – What
- Çəş – Eye
- Çəmə – Our

D:

The letter "D" is pronounced the same as in English, creating a distinct "d" sound.

Examples:

- Das – Hand
- Dəmon – Medicine/Drug
- Dıl – Heart

E:

The letter "E" in Talysh has the sound of "e" as in "men".

Examples:

- Elm – Science
- Ekə – Pour
- Elan/Elon – Advertisement

Ə:

The letter "Ə" represents the sound of "a" as in "bat".

Examples:

- Əv – He
- Əzob – Suffering
- Ədavət – Animosity

F:

The letter "F" produces the sound of "f" as in "foxtrot".

Examples:

- Foydə – Benefit/Use
- Faiz – Interest/Percent
- Fel – Verb

Q:

The letter "Q" in Talysh has the sound of "g" as in "golf".

Examples:

- Qavəlu – Plum
- Qam – Hot
- Qandım – Wheat

Ğ

The letter "Ğ" represents a unique sound that doesn't have an equivalent in the English language. It resembles the Arabic letter "ghayn[1]" or the French "r" sound. This sound is made at the back of the mouth, similar to how "h" is said in English.

Examples:

- Ğab   –   Plate
- Ğavol   –   Drum
- Ğayçi   –   Scissors

H:

The letter "H" is pronounced as "h" in English, creating a distinct "h" sound as in "hot".

Examples:

- Hova   –   Sister
- Hejo   –   Always
- Həvəs   –   Desire

X:

The letter "X" in Talysh doesn't have an equivalent sound in the English language. It is similar to the Russian letter "x," often spelled in English using "k" and "h" combinations, sounding like the "kh" in the Scottish word "loch".

Examples:

- Xıdo   –   God
- Xeyr   –   Benefit/Blessing
- Xaiş   –   Request/Ask

---

1. Arabic غ (غٜن ghayn or ġayn) French "pourquoi".

I:

The letter "I" represents a sound that also doesn't have an equivalent in the English language. It is similar to the Russian letter "ы," often spelled in English as "y", as in "Talysh".

Examples:

- Iştı – Your
- Im – This
- Imvrədə – Here

İ:

The letter "İ" has the sound of "I" as in "bill".

Examples:

- İ – One
- Inotkor – Stubborn
- Imon – Faith

J:

The letter "J" in Talysh doesn't have an equivalent sound in the English language. It is similar to the Russian letter "ж", often spelled in English using "z" and "h" combinations. It is similar to the "j" sound in "pleasure" or "measure".

Examples:

- Jen – Wife/Woman
- Jəgo – Like this
- Jəje – Hedgehog

K:

The letter "K" is pronounced the same as in English, creating a distinct "k" sound.

Examples:

- Kası   –   Turtle
- Kabob   –   Kebab
- Ko   –   Work

L:

The letter "L" has the sound of "l" as in "Lima".

Examples:

- Limo   –   Lemon
- Ləğə   –   Kick
- Lınq   –   Leg

M:

The letter "M" is pronounced the same as in English, creating a distinct "m" sound.

Examples:

- Moy   –   Fish
- Mamu   –   Uncle
- Merd   –   Man

N:

The letter "N" is pronounced the same as in English, creating a distinct "n" sound.

Examples:

- Narıngi – Tangerine
- Namus – Honour
- Ni – No/Isn't

O:

The letter "O" has the sound of "o" as in "open".

Examples:

- Ov – Water
- Oson – Iron
- Oşim/Ovşum – Moon

P:

The letter "P" is pronounced the same as in English, creating a distinct "p" sound.

Examples:

- Pıə – Father
- Pojə – Stick
- Poj – Autumn

R:

The letter "R" has the sound of "r" as in "rainbow".

Examples:

- Ro – Road
- Rang – Colour
- Rozi – Agreeable

S:

The letter "S" is pronounced the same as in English, creating a distinct "s" sound.

Examples:

- Sard – Cold
- Sük – Cockrel
- Sığ – Stone

Ş:

The letter "Ş" produces the sound of "sh" as in "shoe".

Examples:

- Şair – Poet
- Şeir – Poem
- Şin/Şinə – Sweet

T:

The letter "T" is pronounced the same as in English, creating a distinct "t" sound.

Examples:

- Tars – Fear
- Toj – New
- Tı – You (informal)

Ü:

The letter "Ü" has the sound of "ü" as in "Übermensch" or "Uber".

Examples:

- Üzv – Member
- Üfük – Horizon
- Ütü – Iron (device)

V:

The letter "V" produces the sound of "v" as in "verb".

Examples:

- Vıl – Flower
- Vanq/Sədo – Voice
- Varlı(ü) – Rich

Y:

The letter "Y" has the sound of "y" as in "yolk".

Examples:

- Yolə – Big/Grand/Great
- Yod – Memory
- Yetim – Orphan

Z:

The letter "Z" produces the sound of "z" as in "Zulu".

Examples:

- Zıvon – Language
- Zard – Yellow
- Zoə – Son

EXERCISES:

A. Writing in Talysh

Without consulting the book:

1. Write down seven words starting with a vowel (one vowel for each word).
2. Write down ten words starting with a consonant (one consonant for each word).
3. Write down a word denoting colour.
4. Write down a word denoting familial relationship.
5. Write down a word denoting ethnicity.

B. Speaking in Talysh

1. **Salam** – Hello
2. **Çokneiş?** (informal) or **şıma çokneynon?** (formal) – How are you?
3. **Az çokim ve səğ bu. Tı çokneiş?** – I am well, thank you very much. How are you?
4. **Azam çokim ve səğ bu.** I am also well, thank you very much.
5. **Tı kovreyvojiş?** Where are you from?
6. **Az Bədəlonovojim. Tı kovrəyvojiş?** – I am from Badalan. Where are you from?
7. **Az Lankonovojim.** I am from Lankaran.

C. Questions:

1. What is the name of the mountain that runs through the Talysh region?
2. What is the name of the sea that washes the shores of the Talysh region?
3. What dish is the Talysh cuisine famous for?
4. What fruit is the Talysh region known for?

CHAPTER II
NUMERALS

A. Cardinal Numbers

- İ – One
- Dı – Two
- Se – Three
- Ço – Four
- Penc – Five
- Şəş – Six
- Haft – Seven
- Həşt – Eight
- Nəv – Nine
- Da – Ten

In Talysh, numbers from 10 to 20 have individual names:

- Yonzə – Eleven
- Donzə – Twelve
- Senzə – Thirteen
- Çonzə – Fourteen
- Ponzə – Fifteen
- Şonzə – Sixteen
- Havdə – Seventeen
- Həjdə – Eighteen
- Nonzə – Nineteen
- Vist – Twenty

After 20, names of the numbers are expressed by adding an "**o**" to the end of the decimal, followed by the number. For example, **21** will be **vist-o-i**. 22 will be vist-o-di, etc. The names of the decimals are as follows:

- Da — Ten
- Vist — Twenty
- Si — Thirty
- Çıl — Forty
- Penco — Fifty
- Şesto — Sixty
- Hafto — Seventy
- Həşto — Eighty
- Nəve — Ninety
- Sa — Hundred

Numbers after hundred are expressed by adding the decimals with the singulars to the hundred. For example, **hundred twenty-five** will be "**savistopenc**".

Numbers after 199 are expressed by adding singular numbers to the front of the hundred, as follows:

- Di sa — Two hundred
- Se sa — Three hundred
- Ço sa — Four hundred
- Penc sa — Five hundred
- Şəş sa — Six hundred
- Haft sa — Seven hundred
- Həşt sa — Eight hundred
- Nəv sa — Nine hundred
- Həzo — Thousand

Numbers after one thousand are calculated in the same manner by adding a numeral before the thousand, followed by centenary, decimal and singular numbers, for example,

- **Penc həzo penc sa visto se** is five thousand five hundred twenty-three (5,523).
- **Si həzo ço sa hafto şəş** is thirty thousand four hundred seventy-six (30,476).

Numbers from a million follow the same pattern and are expressed as follows:

– 16 –

· Milyon	–	Million
· Milyard	–	Billion
· Trilyon	–	Trillion

B. Ordinal Numbers

Ordinal numbers in Talysh are expressed by adding the ending "mınci" to the end of the number, as follows:

· İmınci	–	First
· Dımınci	–	Second
· Semınci	–	Third
· Çomınci	–	Fourth
· Pencmınci	–	Fifth
· Şəşmınci	–	Sixth
· Haftmınci	–	Seventh
· Həştmınci	–	Eighth
· Nəvmınci	–	Ninth
· Damınci	–	Tenth

EXERCISES:

A. Writing in Talysh

Without consulting the book:

1. Write down three even numbers and three odd numbers.
2. Write down three decimal numbers.
3. Write down three centenary numbers.
4. Write down three ordinal numbers.

Write down the following numbers in words:

1. 25
2. 137
3. 1689
4. 20,879
5. 300,943
6. 1,898,459

B. Speaking in Talysh

1. **Im kon nomrǝe?** – What number is this? [Add your answer in Talysh]
2. **Iştı çand qıla boǝ hıste?** – How many brothers do you have? [Add your answer in Talysh]
3. **Lankonoda çand qılǝ dıyo (deyo) hıste?** – How many seas are in Lankaran? [Add your answer in Talysh]
4. **Tı ıştı pıǝ çanminci zoǝş/kinǝş?** – What number son/daughter are you to your father? [Add your answer in Talysh]

C. Questions

1. How do you say "**first**" in Talysh?
2. How do you say "**eighty**" in Talysh?
3. How do you say "**hundred**" in Talysh?
4. How do you say "**thousand**" in Talysh?
5. How do you say "**million**" in Talysh?

CHAPTER III
PRONOUNS

A. Personal Pronouns

Singular:

- Az/Mı — I
- Tı — You (informal)
- Əv — He/She

Plural:

- Əmə — We
- Şmə — You (formal)
- Əvon — They

B. Possessive Pronouns

Singular:

- Çımı — Mine
- Iştı/bıştə — Your/Yours
- Əçe — His/Hers

Plural:

- Çəmə — Our/Ours
- Şımə — Your/Yours
- Çəvon — Their/Theirs

C. Demonstrative Pronouns

- Im — This
- Ə (v) — That
- Konqlə — Which

– 19 –

D. Interrogative Pronouns

- Ki   –   Who
- Çıki   –   Whose
- Konqlə   –   Which

E. Indefinite Pronouns

- Heç ki   –   No one
- Ve kərə   –   Several

F. Reflexive Pronouns

Singular:

- Az/Mı ıştən)   –   Myself
- Tı ıştən   –   Yourself
- Əv ıştən   –   Himself/Herself/Itself

Plural:

- Əmə ıştən   –   Ourselves
- Şımə ıştən   –   Yourselves
- Əvon ıştən   –   Themselves[2]

G. Reciprocal Pronouns

- Iştəni   –   Each other
- Co qlə   –   One another

EXERCISES:

A. Writing in Talysh

---

2. But note the following structure: "Əmə ıştənəmon kardə – we did it ourselves. Əvon ıştənon kardə – they did it themselves."

– 20 –

Without consulting the book:

1. Write down two personal pronouns (singular and plural).
2. Write down two possessive pronouns (singular and plural).
3. Write down two demonstrative pronouns.
4. Write down two reflexive pronouns.
5. Write down one interrogative and one reciprocal pronoun.

B. Speaking in Talysh

1. **Əv kie?** – Who is he/she/it?
2. **Tı koncoş?** – Where are you? (informal)
3. **Əvon çıki əğlonin?** – Whose kids are they?
4. **Əmə hozomon.** – We are ready.
5. **Im çiçe?** – What is this?
6. **Raxsi bıkə bıştə nənə.** – Dance for your grandmother.
7. **Ki bımi diyəkarda?** – Who is looking after this?
8. **Kongla kinə?** – Which girl?

C. Questions

1. How do you say "**they**" in Talysh?
2. How do you say "**ours**" in Talysh?
3. How do you say "**you**" (informal) in Talysh?
4. How do you say "**mine**" in Talysh?
5. How do you say "**yours**" (formal) in Talysh?

CHAPTER IV
NOUNS

A. Common Nouns

Persons

- Merd – Man[3]
- Jen – Woman
- Zoə – Boy
- Kinə – Girl

- Piə merd – Old man
- Piə jen – Old lady
- Qədə zoə – Little boy
- Qədə kinə – Little girl

- Pıə – Father
- Moa – Mother
- Boə – Brother
- Hovə – Sister

Places:

- Di – Village
- Şəhr – City
- ÖIkə – Country
- Maktab – School
- Vojor – Market

Animals:

- Kıtı – Cat
- Boz – Goat
- Pələnq – Tiger
- Sıpə – Dog

- Kaq – Hen
- Şir – Lion
- Kəse – Turtle
- Xurüz – Rooster

3. In this instance, "man" refers to the male gender. In English, the word "man" can also refer to humanity in general. In Talysh, the word for "human" is "odəm" or "bəşər," without any gender connotation. It encompasses both male and female genders.

– 22 –

- Hırs – Bear
- Bili – Duck
- Ğaz – Goose
- Şəğol – Jackal[4]
- Pəs – Sheep
- Mor – Snake
- Moy – Fish
- Jəj – Hedgehog
- Bəbəzoxl – Frog
- Zandəqo – Cow

Clothing:

- Şəvlo – Trousers
- Kəpot – Skirt
- Şəy – Shirt
- Pencək – Jacket
- Çoxo – Coat
- Əyağqobi – Shoe/s
- Kəloş – Rubber shoes

Fruit:

- Sef – Apple
- Ambu – Pear
- Qavəlu/Əyu – Plum
- Bif – Quince
- Gəysi – Apricot

Vegetables:

- Pamador – Tomato
- lobyə – Bean
- Xıyo – Cucumber
- Kərtov – Potato
- Bodomcon – Eggplant
- Qandım – Wheat

Food & Beverages:

- Nün – Bread
- Nemek – Salt

---

4. In the Badalan village of the Masallı district in the Republic of Azerbaijan, there is a place called "Şəğolakü," which translates to "The hill of jackals".

- Ğənd — Sugar[5]
- Ov — Water
- Çay — Tea
- Polo — Pilaf (Plov[6])
- Ləvəngi — Lavangi[7]
- Tırşinəaş — Tirshinaash[8]

Tools:

- Lapatka — Spade
- Dımrığ — Rake
- Təvə — Axe
- Ərə — Saw
- Çəkıt — Hammer

Time of Day & Seasons:

- Ruj — Day
- Şəv — Night
- Ümrü — Today
- Zinə — Yesterday
- Maşta — Tomorrow
- Maşta – maşta — Early morning
- Şanğo — Evening
- Əvəsor — Spring
- Tovoston — Summer
- Poz — Autumn
- Zomoson — Winter

B. **Proper Nouns**

---

5. If you add "ə" to certain nouns in Talysh, you can form an adjective. For example, "ğənd" (sugar) becomes "ğəndə" (sweet).
6. A rice dish.
7. Stuffed chicken or fish.
8. A type of soup, known as "sour soup" in English (exact translation from Talysh).

Name of Persons:

- İdris   –   Idris
- Eynəli   –   Eynali
- Həsən   –   Hassan
- Gülənbər   –   Gulanbar
- Münəvvər   –   Munavvar

Name of Geographical Locations:

- Lankon   –   Lankaran
- Ostoro   –   Astara
- Lerik   –   Lerik
- Massallü   –   Masalli
- Bədəlon   –   Badalan
- Deyo Xəzər   –   Caspian Sea

C. Concrete Nouns

- Miz   –   Table
- Ustul   –   Chair
- Do   –   Tree
- Maşin   –   Car
- Avtobus   –   Bus

D. Abstract Nouns

- Eşg   –   Love
- Nifrət   –   Hate
- Etibar   –   Trust
- Azad   –   Freedom
- Şocaət   –   Courage

E. Collective Nouns

- Cəmiət   –   Society
- Ailə   –   Family

- Ləşkər   –   Army
- Süri   –   Herd

EXERCISES:

A. Writing in Talysh

Without consulting the book:

1. Write down five common nouns.
2. Write down two abstract nouns.
3. Write down two collective nouns.
4. Write down two concrete nouns.

B. Speaking in Talysh

1. **Iştı piə nom çiçe?** – What is your father's name?
2. **Saat çande?** – What time is it?
3. **Im pamador tojae?** – Is this tomato fresh?
4. **Im çıki kıtıe?** – Whose cat is this?
5. **Əçi etibarış ni** – He/she is not trustworthy.
6. **Ujan poz omeda livon xəzone** – Autumn has arrived once again, and yellow leaves are everywhere.
7. **Şanğo bə kovra bəşemon?** – Where shall we go this evening?
8. **Im cəmiyyət azad(ozod) ni** – This society is not free.[9]

C. Questions

1. How do you say "**Caspian Sea**" in Talysh?
2. How do you say "**my sister**" in Talysh?
3. How do you say "**black trousers**" in Talysh?
4. How do you say "**my love**" in Talysh?
5. How do you say "**red apple**" in Talysh?

---

9. Meaning the freedom of the society is limited or restricted.

CHAPTER V
ADJECTIVES

A. Descriptive Adjectives

Colours:

- Sipi   –   White
- Zard   –   Yellow
- Syo   –   Black
- Sı   –   Red
- Kavu   –   Blue
- Boz   –   Green

Examples:

1. Sipiə vıl   –   White flower
2. Syo çəş   –   Black eye
3. Sıə pamador   –   Red tomato
4. Zardə mu   –   Blonde

Size:

- Yola   –   Big/Great
- Qədəli   –   Small
- Barz   –   Tall
- Nızım   –   Short

Examples:

1. Əv yola zoəe   –   He is a big boy.
2. Çımı əğıl qədəliye   –   My kid is small (i.e. My child is young)
3. Im miz nızıme   –   This table is short (i.e. This table is small)

Taste:

- Şin   –   Sweet
- Sü   –   Salty
- Tel   –   Bitter
- Tıj   –   Hot/spicy
- Tırš   –   Sour

Examples:

1. Kon meyvə şine?   –   Which fruit is sweet?
2. Im polo ve süe   –   This pilav is very salty.
3. Im sef tırşe   –   This apple is sour.

Temperature:

- Qam   –   Hot
- Sard   –   Cold
- İlığ   –   Warm
- Sərin   –   Cool

Examples:

1. Londonadə həvo çokneye, qame ya sarde?   –   How is the weather in London, hot or cold?
2. Çımı çay ilığe   –   My tea is warm.
3. Isa qame şəv sərin bəbe   –   It is hot now. It will be cooler in the evening.

Attitude:

- Xoşbəxt   –   Happy
- Nədim   –   Naughty
- Rıkin   –   Angry
- Rəhmsiz   –   Ruthless
- Bezu   –   Helpless

- Behəyo – Shameless
- Məsuliyətsiz – Irresponsible
- Mehribon – Kind

Examples:

1. Çımı xoşbəxtə rujon koncoe? – Where are my happy days?
2. Ümrü əv ve rıkine – Today he is very angry.
3. Imkansızlığ odəmi bezu kardə – Lack of finance makes one helpless.

Distance:

- Nez – Close
- Diaro – Far

Examples:

1. Əçi kə neze – His house is close by.
2. Diaro şedəş? – Are you going far?

B. Demonstrative Adjectives

- Im – This
- Ə – That
- Imon – These
- Ivon – Those

Examples:

1. Im çiçe? – What is this?
2. Ə ıştı asbe? – Is that your horse?

C. Possessive Adjectives:

- Çımı – My/mine

- Çəmə   –   Our/Ours
- Iştı   –   Your/Yours(singular)
- Şımə   –   Your/Yours (plural)
- Əçe   –   His/Hers
- Çəvon   –   Their/Theirs

Examples:

1. Im çımı maşine   –   This is my car.

2. Əv şımə əğıle?   –   Is that your child?

3. Bəşdə baba maç bıdə   –   Give a kiss to your grandfather.

D. Quantitative Adjectives

- Həmə   –   All
- Qıley/filon   –   Some/Certain
- İtkə   –   A little
- Ve   –   Many

Examples:

1. Həmə vottən jağo bıkə joğo bıkə   –   Everyone says, "do it this way or that way".

2. Filon vrədə vottən qıle yola dıyo hıste   –   They say there is a big sea in a certain place.

3. Əçe ve problem hıste   –   He has too many problems.

E. Interrogative Adjectives

- Konqla   –   Which
- Ki   –   Which one
- Çıki   –   Whose
- Çi/çiç   –   What

Examples:

1. Kongla alim votəşe "zamon nisbiye"? – Which scientist said, "time is relative"?
2. Bə çıki ğırməğ külmə omə? – Whose fishing rod has hooked a fish?

F. Indefinite Adjectives

- Xeyli – Quite a few/A lot
- Ha – Each/Every
- Çand qıla – Several
- Ve – Many
- Kali – Few/A few
- Kali qıla – Some

Examples:

1. Ha tərəf sıə vıle – There are red flowers everywhere.
2. Əv xeyli fikr kardə – He/She thinks a lot.

EXERCISES:

A. Writing in Talysh

Without consulting the book:

1. Write down five descriptive adjectives.
2. Write down three demonstrative adjectives.
3. Write down three possessive adjectives.
4. Write down three quantitative adjectives.
5. Write down two interrogative adjectives.
6. Write down two indefinite adjectives.

B. Speaking in Talysh

1. **Ov çokneye?** – How is the water? [Add a response in Talysh]
2. **Əv yola merde?** – Is he a big man? [Add a response in Talysh]
3. **Az İtkə ro şedəm, bə tı?** – I am walking a short distance. How about you? [Add a response in Talysh]
4. **Çəmə əğlon dərs handən?** – Are our kids studying? [Add a response in Talysh]
5. **İm çie?** – What is it? [Add a response in Talysh]

C. Questions
1. How do you say "**blue**" in Talysh?
2. How do you say "**yours** (plural)" in Talysh?
3. How do you say "**whose**" in Talysh?
4. How do you say "**kind**" in Talysh?
5. How do you say "**shameless**" in Talysh?

CHAPTER VI
ADVERBS

A. Adverbs of Manner

- Rə — Quickly
- Asüdə — Calmly
- Qədə – qədə — Slowly
- Ehtiyotli — Carefully
- Səbrli — Patiently
- Gəšəng — Beautifully
- Həkimonə — Scholarly
- Natiqanə — Eloquently

Examples:

1. Avtobus rə omə — The bus came quickly.
2. Ehtiyotli bobiš salomət bəbiš — If you are careful, you will be safe.
3. Asüdə bıvot — Speak slowly.

B. Adverbs of Frequency

- Hakənə — Sometimes
- Hejo — Always
- Heç vaxt — Never
- Rə – rə — Often
- Kam — Rarely
- Bəzən — Sometimes

C. Adverbs of time

- Isə — Now
- Zinə — Yesterday
- Ümrü — Today
- Maşta — Tomorrow
- Bı nezondə — Soon
- Pešo — Later

Examples:

1. Pešo boy — Come later.
2. Zinə vottəme ümrü qam bəbe — I said yesterday it would be hot today.
3. Maşta bə kovrə bəşeş? — Where are you going tomorrow?

D. Adverbs of Place

- Ivrədə — Here
- Əvrədə — There
- Havrədə — Everywhere
- Heçvrədə — Nowhere
- Kovrədə? — Where?
- Bəzivradə — Somewhere

Examples:

1. Az tınim kovrədə vində — I have seen you somewhere.
2. Heç vrədə bə odəmi rohəti ni — Nowhere is there peace for man.
3. Ti əvrədə çiç kardəş? — What are you doing there?

E. Adverbs of Degree

- Ve — Very/A lot
- İtkə/qədə/kami — A little
- Həni — More/Anymore
- Kifayət qədər — Enough
- Tamum — Completely

Examples:

1. Az şonım ve pidəme – I like honey a lot.
2. Kam sxan bıka – Do not talk too much.
3. Az həni tınım pidəm ni – I don't like you anymore.
4. Əv Londoni tamum tərkış karde – He/She left London completely.

F. Interrogative Adverbs

- Çiç – What
- Keynə – When
- Biçi – Why
- Çokne – How
- Kovrə – Where

Examples:

1. Tı çiç kardəş? – What are you doing?
2. Əv keynə bomə? – When will he/she come?
3. Tı biçi jəğo vottəş? – Why do you say that?
4. Bə kovrə şedəş? – Where are you going?

G. Conjunctive Adverbs

- Əçesən əlavə – Moreover
- Fikr dıdamon – Nevertheless
- Həmçinin – Also
- Bıçimiqora – Therefore
- Əncəğ – However

Examples:

1. Az Badalonda muada bam bıçimiqora az tolushi zondam — I was born in Badalan, therefore, I know Talysh.
2. Az həmçinin Inglisian zondam — I also speak English.
3. Az vittəm və əçesən əlavə dənıştəm — I run; moreover, I swim.

EXERCISES:

A. Writing in Talysh

Without consulting the book:

1. Write down three adverbs of manner.
2. Write down three adverbs of frequency.
3. Write down three adverbs of time.
4. Write down three adverbs of place.
5. Write down three adverbs of degree.
6. Write down three interrogative adverbs.
7. Write down three interrogative adverbs.
8. Write down three conjunctive adverbs.

B. Speaking in Talysh

1. **Bə di çoknəy bışamon?** – How shall we get to the village? [Add a response in Talysh]
2. **Əv bə tı keynə zangış kardə?** – When did he/she call you? [Add a response in Talysh]
3. **Vo kovrədən omedə?** – Where does the draft come from? [Add a response in Talysh]
4. **Çəmə əğıl ve sxan kardə** – Our kid talks a lot. [Add a response in Talysh]
5. **Tı biçi joğo məsuliyyətsıziş?** – Why are you so irresponsible? [Add a response in Talysh]

C. Questions

1. How do you say "**quickly**" in Talysh?
2. How do you say "**where**" in Talysh?
3. How do you say "**tomorrow**" in Talysh?
4. How do you say "**kind**" in Talysh?
5. How do you say "**enough**" in Talysh?

CHAPTER VII
VERBS

A. Present Tense

In Talysh, verb tenses are simpler compared to the English language. The Talysh language primarily has three tenses: Present, Past, and Future.

Let's explore some examples using the verbs "to see" and "to speak." This will give you a better understanding of how these verbs are expressed in Talysh, with different pronouns.

To See:

- Az vindəm   –   I see
- Əmə vindəmon   –   We see
- Tı vindəş   –   You (singular) see
- Şımə vindon   –   You see (plural)
- Əv vində   –   He/She sees
- Əvon vindən   –   They see

To Speak:

- Az sıxan kardəm   –   I speak
- Əmə sıxan kardəmon   –   We speak
- Tı sıxan kardəş   –   You (singular) speak
- Şımə sıxan kardon   –   You (plural) speak
- Əv sıxan kardə   –   He/She speaks
- Əvon sıxan kardən   –   They speak

B. Past Tense

In Talysh, the past tense is expressed by adding various endings to verbs. These endings are determined by the type of pronoun used in a sentence (Az (I) vind (verb) ıme (ending that attaches to the first pronoun I).

– 38 –

Let's look at some examples below:

- Az vindıme   –   I saw
- Əmə vindemone   –   We saw
- Tı vinde   –   You (singular) saw
- Şımə-vindone   –   You (plural) saw
- Əy vindışe   –   He/She saw
- Əvon vindışone   –   They saw

Additionally, in some cases, the Past Tense can be formed by adding the endings "bish," "bim," "be," or "bin" to the verb. For example, "I was asleep" is expressed as "Az hıtabim".

- Az hıtabim   –   I was asleep
- Əmə hıtabimon –   We were asleep
- Tı hıtabiş   –   You (singular) were asleep
- Şımə hıtabion   –   You (plural) were asleep
- Əv hıtabe   –   He/She was asleep
- Əvon hıtabin   –   They were asleep

C. **Future Tense**

In Talysh, the future tense is formed by adding specific prefixes and endings to the verb. The choice of prefix and ending depends on the pronoun used. For example, "I will go" is expressed as "Az bəşem". "We will go" is expressed as "Əmə bəşemon".

Let's look at some more examples:

- Az bəşem   –   I will go
- Əmə bəşemon   –   We will go
- Tı bəşeş   –   You (singular) will go
- Şımə bəşeon   –   You (plural) will go
- Əv bəşe   –   He/She will go
- Əvon bəşen   –   They will go

EXERCISES:

A. Writing in Talysh

Without consulting the book:

1. Write down three verbs in the present tense.
2. Write down five verbs in the past tense.
3. Write down three verbs in the future tense.

B. Speaking in Talysh

1. **Tı vinde əv çiçeş[10] karde?** – You saw what he did? [Add a response in Talysh]
2. **Tı bə kovra bəşeş?** – Where will you go? [Add a response in Talysh]
3. **Çay pidə?** – Would you like some tea? [Add a response in Talysh]

C. Questions

1. How do you say "**I sing**" in Talysh?
2. How do you say "**I cried**" in Talysh?
3. How do you say "**I will come tomorrow**" in Talysh?

---

10. Note the word "what" changes depending on the pronoun preceding it eg. "Az çiçım kardə" - What I did. "Əvon çiçışon kardə" - What they did.

CHAPTER VIII
OTHER PARTS OF SPEECH

A. Conjunctions

In Talysh, conjunctions are used to connect words, phrases, or clauses. Here are some examples of conjunctions and their meanings:

- Və – And
- Əmo/əncəğ – But
- Ya – Or
- Hələ/ujnən – Yet

Examples:

1. Asb və sıpa – A horse and a dog.

2. Az bə tı qıle sxan bavotem əncəğ be heçki məvot – I will tell you something, but don't tell anyone.

3. Hələ sol omə külmə oma ni – A little fish has arrived, but a big fish has not arrived yet.

B. Prepositions

Prepositions in Talysh indicate relationships between words in a sentence. They can be expressed by single words or by combining various nouns and endings.

Let's look at some examples:

- Sə/səpe – On
- Peşton/peşt – Behind
- De – With
- Aradə – Between

– 41 –

Examples:

1. Nemek koncoe? – Where is the salt?
   Mizi səpedə   On the table.
2. Az peşton   – I stayed behind.
   mandəm
3. Çəvon aradə   – There is a
   narazılığ hıste   disagreement
                      between them.

The preposition "in" in Talysh is formed by adding an ending to a noun. For example, "in the house" is expressed as "kədə" ("kə" for house, "də" for in).

Here are a few more examples:

1. Bukuədə   –   In Baku[11]
2. Çımı dılədə –   In my heart[12]
3. Hayotədə   –   In life

C. Interjections

Interjections in Talysh are used to express emotions, reactions, or exclamations. Here are some examples:

- Vay   – Oh no!
- Vay   – Oops!
- Vay dədə   – Wow!
- Afərin   – Well done
- Bijjoş   – May you live long/well done
- Ey gidə merd – Oy-oy big man!

---

11. Capital of Azerbaijan
12. Note that in the phrase "dıl" meaning "heart," the ending added to it is "ədə" and not "də." This variation occurs depending on whether the noun ends with a consonant or a vowel. Words ending with a consonant attract the former version, while words ending with a vowel attract the latter version.

Examples:

1. Vay çımı polo sütə ki! — Oh no, my pilaf has burned!
2. Afərin bə tı! — Well done to you!
3. Ey gidə merd, zondəş tı çiç kardəş! — Oy oy big man, you know what you do!

EXERCISES:

A. Writing in Talysh

Without consulting the book:

1. Write down three conjunctions.
2. Write down three prepositions.
3. Write down three interjections.

B. Speaking in Talysh

1. **Nün kıve?** – Where is the bread? (Respond in Talysh: "On the table".)
2. **Çəmə kəy peşton çiç hıste?** – What is behind our house? (Respond in Talysh: "There is a beautiful garden behind our house".)
3. **Bijjoş! Hər zəmon joğo zirək bıbu** – Well done! May you always be so potent/productive.

C. Questions

1. How do you say "**inside the house**" in Talysh?
2. How do you say "**but**" in Talysh?
3. How do you say "**well done**" in Talysh?

CHAPTER IX
SYNTAX

In Talysh, words in sentences follow a specific order. Let's explore some examples below:

- Az (pronoun) şedəm (verb) bə (preposition "to") kə (noun) – I am going home.

Generally, it is not possible to change the positions of the parts of speech in Talysh. However, there are exceptions. For instance, if we remove the pronoun from the above sentence, the structure will be as follows:

- "Şedəm bə kə" – This will still be interpreted as "I am going home" because the first-person singular is implied in the verb's ending.

More examples:

- Bışəmon bə kə? – Shall we go home?

- Bə kovrə bışəmon? – Where shall we go?

- Çiç pidə[13]? – What do you want?

- Az bə tı nıvote[14]? – Did I not tell you?

- Ümrü bə kovrə bışəmon? – Where shall we go today?

---

13. The word "pidə" in Talysh consists of two linguistic components. Its first ingredient is the verb "to want". The second ingredient is the pronoun, which is expressed through the ending "ə".

14. In Talysh, the negative form is expressed by adding the prefix "nı" to the beginning of the verb. Additionally, the ending of the word may change. For example, "az vottame/vottabim" is the past tense of the verb "to say", meaning "I said". The past tense of the negative form, "did I not tell you?", would be "az bə tı nivote?"

- Bıvot[15] çiçe pidə - Say, what is it that you want?

- Səbrım mandə ni (səbr noun "patience") ("ım" an ending expressing pronoun "my") mandə ("mandə" verb "left" "ni" "not") - I have no patience left.

- Əğiliş? - Are you a kid?

- Tı əğiliş - You are a kid.

- Əğıl məbu - Don't be a kid (i.e. Don't be naïve)

- Omedəş? - Are you coming?

- Dımı hənək məkə[16] - Do not play with me.

Here are some more examples with varied sentence structures:

- Maştə-maştə ("early in the morning") əvon ("they") çiç (what) kardən (do) əyo (there) az (I) zondə (know) nim (not) - I have no idea what they are doing there so early.

- Əzoniş ("you can't know") şon ("honey") harde ("to eat") nikaşoş ("to undertake") zəhmət ("hard work") - You can't taste honey if you do not work hard for it.

- Bədə (bad) ro (road) əşenimon[17] (won't we walk on) - We will not pursue inequitable paths.

---

15. In Talysh, the prefix "bı" is added to a verb to express an instruction or command to do something. For example, "bivot" means "say". On the other hand, to express the negative form, meaning "don't do it," the prefix "mə" is used. For instance, "məvot" means "don't say." Similarly, "bıkə" means "do",and "məkə" means "don't".

16. Dı (with) mı (me) hənək (play) məkə (don't).

17. In this sentence, the word "əşenimon" serves multiple functions. The prefix "ə" indicates "will not" or "shall not". "Şe" is a verb, which, in this case, represents the neutral form of the verb "to walk." "Ni" is a suffix meaning "no". Lastly, "mon" is an ending denoting the pronoun "we".

- 45 -

· Çoka (good) merd (man) be (being) ve (very) çətine (difficult) – Being a good man is very difficult.

EXERCISES:

A. Writing in Talysh

Without consulting the book:

1. Write down three sentences starting with pronouns.
2. Write down three sentences starting with a noun.
3. Write down three sentences starting with an adverb.

B. Speaking in Talysh

1. **Bə mı dyəkə** – Look at me [Add a response in Talysh – "Yes, how can I help?"]
2. **Az ıştı roədə kəşeme həsrət** – I have missed you [Add a response in Talysh – I have missed you, too].
3. **Dınyo bo tı hənəke?** – Life is a game for you? [Add a response in Talysh – "No, it is not"]

c. Questions

1. How do you say "**let's go home**" in Talysh?
2. How do you say "**I am not interested in playing**" in Talysh?
3. How do you say "**it is late, I want to sleep**" in Talysh?

– 46 –

CHAPTER X
DIRECT AND INDIRECT SPEECH, CODITIONAL SENTENCES

A. DIRECT & INDIRECT SPEECH

Direct

Əv vottə "Az ov pidəme" – He says, "I want water".

Əvon vottən "ve die, bə kə boşamon?" – They say, "it's late, shall we go home?

Əmə bə tı nevıtomone "əmə pidəmon ni?" – Didn't we tell you, "we do not want it?"

Tı vote "az bomem" – You said, "I will come".

Indirect

Əv vottə əv ovış pidə – He says he wants water.

Əvon vottən lazım ni – They say there is no need for it.

Tı vote tı bomeş – You said you would come.

B. CONDITIONAL SENTENCES

Əgər (if) tı (you) bəşeş (go) azəm (I too) bomem (will come) – If you go, I will also come.

Həvo (weather) qam(warm) bobo (to be) bəşemon (will be going) bə (to) diyo (sea) – If the weather is hot, we will go to the beach.

Əgər (if) zonambe (I had known) tı (you) joğo (like this) bebəfoiş (untrustworthy) bə (to) tı (you) etibar (trust) nəkardim (I would not) – Had I known you are so unreliable, I would not have trusted you.

EXERCISES:

A. Writing in Talysh

Without consulting the book:

1. Give three examples of direct speech.
2. Give three examples of indirect speech.
3. Give three examples of conditional speech.

B. Speaking in Talysh

1. **Əv vottə "əğlon çiç vottən?"** – He says, "what do the kids say?" [Turn this into indirect speech in Talysh"]
2. **Az vottəm "harde pidəm ni"** – I said, "I do not want to eat". [Turn this into indirect speech in Talysh].
3. **ə kinə vottə "dərs hande ve çətine"** – That girl says studying is very hard. [Turn this into indirect speech in Talysh]

C. Questions

1. How do you say **"if you study, you can play"** in Talysh?
2. How do you say **"if it were easy, everyone would do it"** in Talysh?
3. How do you say **"unless you eat your food, you can't go out"** in Talysh?

CHAPTER XI
GLOSSARY

A. THE HUMAN BODY

Sə – Head	Dıl – Heart
Das – Hand	Lıpüt – Lip
Vek – Kidney	Peşt – Back
Mu – Hair	Jiqər – Liver
Angıştə – Finger	Zıvon – Tongue
Rijə – Lungs	Lıng – Leg/foot
Təvil – Forehead	Poşnə – Heel
Düş/Am – Shoulder	Dandon – Tooth
Rüə – Guts	Nangır – Nail
Çəş[18] – Eye	Zno – Knee
Sinə – Chest	Gi – Neck
Mədə – Stomach	Əzələ – Muscle
Vıni – Nose	Çonə – Jaw/Chin
Poşton – Breast	Bəv – Brow
Damar – Vessels	Dim/Rü – Face
Guş – Ear	Mijə – Eyelash
Lüz/Ləvə[19] –Belly/Stomach	Kəş – Arm

B. FAMILY

Pıə – Father	Xalə – Aunt (maternal)
Baba – Grandfather	Buə – Brother
Bibi – Aunt (paternal)	Mamu/Amu – Uncle (paternal)
Muə/dodo – Mother	Hova – Sister
Nənə – Grandmother	Dayi – Uncle (maternal)

---

18. In Talysh, the plural form of words is typically expressed by adding the ending "on" to the noun. For example, "çəş" means "eye," while "çəşon" represents the plural form "eyes." Similarly, "əğıl" means "child," and "əğlon" is used for the plural form "children."

19. The famous Talysh dish "ləvəngi" (which means stuffed in the belly) derives its name from the word "ləvəng".

– 49 –

The word "cousin" in Talysh is expressed by combining the words uncle and aunty with the words "zoə" (son) and 'kinə" (daughter). For example, bibi kinə (female paternal cousin), dayi zoə (male maternal cousin).

C. BUILDINGS

Kə	–	House
Kümə	–	Stable
Məktəb	–	School
Tualet/zaxod	–	Toilet
Məscid	–	Mosque
Həmom	–	Bathroom
Xəstəxonə	–	Hospital

D. PROFESSIONS

Doxtor	–	Doctor
Pırəkürür	–	Public Prosecutor
Müəllim	–	Teacher
Əktyor	–	Actor
Vəkil	–	Lawyer
Polis	–	Police
Arxitekt	–	Architect
Məlo/Axund	–	Cleric
Bənno	–	Builder
Hakim	–	Judge

E. GEOGRAPHY

Kuçə	–	Street
Ru	–	River
Sahə	–	Field
Qəsəbə	–	District
Göl/Xıl	–	Lake
Band	–	Mountain
Di	–	Village
Dyo	–	Sea
Vişə	–	Forest

Şəhr	–	City
Okyan	–	Ocean
Şəlolə	–	Waterfall
ÖIkə	–	Country
Qitə	–	Continent

F. COUNTRIES

Azərbaycan	–	Azerbaijan
Ingilistan	–	England
Urüsyət	–	Russia
Pakistan	–	Pakistan
Türkiyə	–	Turkey
Israil	–	Israel
Iron	–	Iran
Səudiyyə	–	Saudi Arabia
Əmrikə	–	America (U.S.A)
Fransa	–	France

G. SPORTS

Futbol	–	Football
Şahmat	–	Chess
Boks	–	Boxing
Reqbi	–	Rugby
Dəçike	–	Wrestling
Qimnastika	–	Gymnastics
Tenis	–	Tennis
MMA	–	MMA
Şınov	–	Swimming
Şaşki	–	Chequers

H. FOOD & DRINK

Nün	–	Bread
Makaron	–	Pasta
Kaşa	–	Porridge
Nemek	–	Salt
Məkə	–	Corn

Ləvəngi	–	A dish[20]
Ğənd	–	Sugar
Qəhvə	–	Coffee
Aş	–	Soup
Şon	–	Honey
Bibər	–	Hot chili/Pepper
Polo	–	Pilaf
Bırz	–	Rice
Rüyən	–	Butter
Bozbaş	–	Stew
Ov	–	Water
Tort/Keks	–	Cake
Qüjd	–	Meat
Çay	–	Tea
Pəni	–	Cheese
Kag	–	Chicken
Limonad	–	Lemonade
Cır	–	Cottage cheese
Moğna	–	Egg
Ərəğ	–	Vodka
Sirkə badımcon	–	Pickled aubergines
Moy	–	Fish

I. **ASTROPHYSICS**

Səma/Osmon	–	Sky
Ovşum	–	Moon
Həşi	–	Sun
Astovə	–	Star
Kosmos	–	Cosmos
Qalaktika	–	Galaxy
Kainat	–	Universe

---

20. Stuffed chicken, fish, turkey etc.

J. SUBJECTS

Fəlsəfə	–	Philosophy
Astrofizika	–	Astrophisics
Fizika	–	Physics
Ingilisə zıvon	–	English
Ədəbiyyat	–	Literature
Musiği	–	Music
Həndəsə	–	Geometry
Kimya	–	Chemistry
Cəbr	–	Mathematics
Tarix	–	History
Anatomya	–	Anatomy
Bioloqiya	–	Biology

K. TIME

Keçmış	–	Past
Isa	–	Present
Gələcək	–	Future
Rə	–	Early
Di	–	Late

CHAPTER XII
TALYSH CULTURE

A. POETRY

Talysh poetry shares similarities with Azeri and Persian poetry in terms of structure and style. It incorporates different rhyming structures and varying lengths of sentences in a verse. Here are some examples:

Kəvələyim kəvələ.	I am a chubby bird.
Iman qüjde bə şələ	I have lots of meat.
Patəkəsni dız nıbu.	If the chef weren't a thief.
Nəve kəse qatığe[21]	I could have fed 90 people.

This is a simple structure, containing seven clauses. In this type of verse, the first, second, and fourth sentences rhyme with each other, while the third sentence is different. In Talysh poetry, there are several poetic structures in addition to the one mentioned above.

Həğiğət bə vırədə.	Truth is here.
Zü əvini zərədə	Force can't be used on a gem.
Çətinədə, darədə	In difficulty and trouble.
Qıryət bikəşonemon	We are honourable.
Əmə, Toloşonemon	We are the Talysh

In this type of structure, the first three sentences rhyme with each other, and the last two also rhyme with each other. The fifth sentence serves as the core rhyming sentence, with the word "Toloşonemon" being the rhyming word. The last word in the fourth sentence must rhyme with this word.

Çəşiku ars omedə kəşiku sard omedə
Tıni gin kardə rujo dardisə dard omedə
Dınyoku sı nıbemon dı eşği pi nıbemon
Hama ba arzu rasayn əməysə ı nıbemon

---

21. My paternal grandmother used to sing this song to me when I was a child. Apparently, I was very chubby, and this is a song that Talysh women usually sing to chubby kids in the family.

In this structure, there are 14 clauses. This represents a more complex verse structure found in Azeri, Talysh, Persian, and Arabic[22] poetry. In this structure, the first sentence rhymes with the second, and the third sentence rhymes with the fourth.

> Be tı mande bomono ve yolə darde.
> Çımı xoşbəxtə rüjon tı dişta barde.

In this structure, there are 12 clauses.

There are several other structures in Talysh poetry that feature varying numbers of clauses and different rhyming patterns. Among them, the most complex structure is called "Ğəzəl". This structure typically consists of 14 to 15 clauses and incorporates several pairs of long sentences. The final sentence of each pair rhymes with the rhyming sentence.

> Eşği zil voşnə tı vindəm ve kaxobon dılədə.
> Az qıle doğba kabobim çə kabobon dılədə.[23]

> Be tı doğbəm besütəm kəştəm əzobon iyənə.
> Şinə orozoş bomo anandə əzobon dılədə.

B. **MUSIC**

Talysh songs predominantly express emotions like love, sorrow, nostalgia, patriotism, and friendship. One of the most famous Talysh songs is called "Zangi Yarim," which was performed by the renowned Azerbaijani singer, Rashid Bebutov. Here is a verse from the song:

---

22. Verses with sentences containing more than 12 clauses are considered complex sentences, known as "Vazn," and they are referred to as "Əruz".
23. The first two sentences in a ğəzəl (a poetic form) are rhyming sentences, and the last sentence in subsequent pairs always rhymes with the initial rhyming sentence.

Dasədəm tovə
Tı çımı xanımə hovə
Zəngi yarım, zəngi yarım
Çe ğəşənge

Nənə bəştı ğıbon.
Şərəbani, mərəbani.
Co kasi həmro.

Zəngi yarım, zəngi yarım
Çe ğəşənge

Another well-known Talysh song is,
"Ay Çımı Dilbər," which translates
to "Oh My Beloved" in English.

Ay çımı dilbər
Con çımı dilbər

Mı ditım sə karde
Çımı dıli arzü
Çımı dildə mande

C. **PROVERBS**

Sıpə dümi bıburuş pəs əvini – If you cut a
dog's tail, it won't become a sheep[24].

Dıyo bə sıpə qəvi mordol ni ki – The sea
will not be marred by a dog's mouth[25].

Bə tı bılbıl bıhando ya küəzing fərq ni – It
makes no difference to you whether it's the
calling of a nightingale or a yellow finch[26].

24. This means that you cannot fundamentally change someone or something by making minor alterations.
25. This means that small things will not have a significant impact on larger things.
26. This means that the person to whom it is addressed is either ignorant or ungrateful.

Filə fikir kardə, filəvonam fikir kardə! –
An elephant has been thinking without
knowing his rider has also been thinking.[27]

Hələ sol omə külmə omə ni – A small
fish has arrived, not a big one.[28]

---

27   This means that the addressee is not the only one capable of thinking; there are others who are better at it than the addressee.

28   This means that the problem you are currently facing is not the most severe; there are bigger challenges yet to come.

CHAPTER XIII
SIMILARITIES WITH OTHER SANSCRITIC LANGUAGES

A. **Talysh**

Ov – Water
Dıl – Heart
Sard – Cold
Nün – Bread
Dandun – Tooth
Ko – Work

Qam – Hot
Nemek – Salt
Çəş – Eye
Kü – Mountain
Qandom – Wheat
Mu – Hair

B. **Farsi**

Ab – Water
Del – Heart
Sard[31] – Old
Nan – Bread
Dandon[32] – Tooth
Kar – Work

Qarm[29] – Hot
Namak[30] – Salt
Cheshm – Eye
Kuh – Mountain
Qandom[33] – Wheat
Mu – Hair

C. **Zaza**[34]

Aw – Water
Qelb – Heart
Serd/Serdo – Cold
Nan – Bread
Dıldan – Tooth
Kar/Gürwe – Work

Germ – Hot
Sol – Salt
Çım – Eye
Ko – Mountain
Xelle/Ğelle – Wheat
Por – Hair

---

29. "a" is pronounced as "a" in apple.
30. As above.
31. As above.
32. As above
33. As above. In Talysh "a" pronounced as "a" in art.
34. Zaza are the closest ethnic group to Talysh.

D. **Kurdish (Kirmanji)**

Av – Water
Dil – Heart
Sarma – Cold
Nan – Bread
Diran – Tooth
Kar – Work

Germa – Hot
Xwê – Salt
Çav – Eye
Çîya – Mountain
Gennim – Wheat
Por – Hair

E. **Hindi/Urdu**

Paani – Water
Dil – Heart
Thanda – Cold
Roti – Bread
Danth –Tooth
Kaam – Work

Garam – Hot
Namak – Salt
Ankh – Eye
Pahad – Mountain
Gehoon – Wheat
Baal – Hair

Afterword

With a passion to educate and share my knowledge, I originally set out to write this book with the intention of helping others who have a desire to learn the Talysh language, particularly those whose first language is English. However, as I began to work on the book's content, collaborating with family and friends who continue to reside within the Talysh region of Azerbaijan, I also wanted to put the Talysh people on the global radar and raise awareness of their long-standing heritage and unique cultural traditions.

As you embed the Talysh language into your skillset, I hope you continue to reference this book and share your insights with others. It has been a real pleasure exploring my own cultural heritage again and reconnecting with the language I was taught as a child by my grandparents, and so I thank you for your commitment and interest in keeping the Talysh language alive.

Rauf Khalilov

About the Author

Rauf Khalilov is a lawyer by profession, having founded Mergul Law in 2013. He lives and works in London, UK, and is married with two children. His cultural heritage can be traced directly back to Azerbaijan, and specifically the Talysh people, having been born in the south of the country, where his paternal family are from.

When Rauf is not working or spending time with his family, he enjoys writing books, poetry, and music, as well as cooking, and teaching children P.E. and chess at a Sunday School. As well as this book, Rauf has also written two children's books, with all proceeds from the book sales going to children in need. The first book is titled, "The Legend of Sidri", and the second is titled, "Mimi", which raises awareness of autism. Rauf also speaks eight languages, including Talysh, Russian, Azeri and Farsi. In the future, Rauf has a desire to become a Judge.

Milton Keynes UK
Ingram Content Group UK Ltd.
UKHW020628300424
441957UK00007B/24